Cambridge Early Years

Mathematics

Learner's Book 2A

Alison Borthwick & Cherri Moseley

Contents

Note to parents and practitioners   3

Block 1: Friends, family and me   4

Block 2: Home and buildings   18

Acknowledgements   32

Note to parents and practitioners

This Learner's Book provides activities to support the first term of Mathematics for Cambridge Early Years 2.

Activities can be used at school or at home. Children will need support from an adult. Additional guidance about activities can be found in the **For practitioners** boxes.

Children will encounter the following characters within this book. You could ask children to point to the characters when they see them on the pages, and say their names.

The Learner's Book activities support the Teaching Resource activities. The Teaching Resource provides step-by-step coverage of the Cambridge Early Years curriculum and guidance on how the Learner's Book activities develop the curriculum learning statements.

Hi, my name is Mia.

Find us on the front covers doing lots of fun activities.

Hi, my name is Gemi.

Hi, my name is Rafi.

Hi, my name is Kiho.

Block 1 — Friends, family and me

How many fish?
Colour and count.

For practitioners
Children colour the fish. Use the numeral 5 to help children make a connection between the picture and the number. Encourage children to count the fish.
Use this as an opportunity to remind children of the *Once I Caught a Fish Alive* rhyme.

Spiders on the web

Draw and count.

Draw 6 spiders on the web.

For practitioners

Children draw the spiders on the web. Encourage children to count the spiders they have drawn. Once all 6 spiders are on the web, cover some of the spiders with a piece of paper and encourage children to count up to different numbers, e.g., 4, 2, 3, 5.

Rocket countdown!
Colour and count.

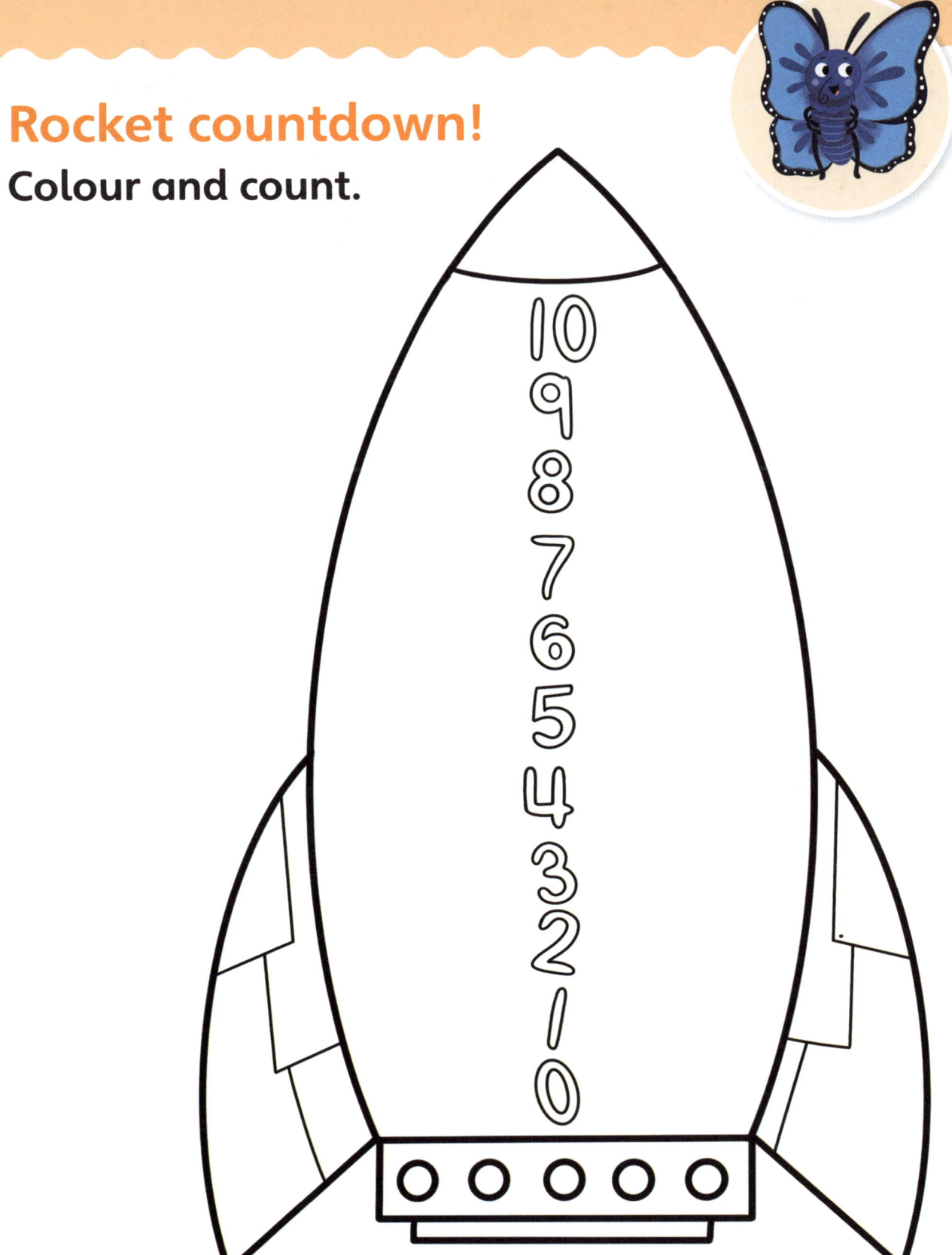

For practitioners
Children colour the numbers 0 to 10 on the rocket.
Encourage children to count backwards from 10 once they reach the top of the rocket.

0, 1, 2, 3!
Write and say.

0   0   0

1   1   1

2   2   2

3   3   3

For practitioners
Children practise writing numbers 0, 1, 2 and 3. Children say aloud the numbers they have written.

4, 5, 6, 7!
Write and say.

4   4   4

5   5   5

6   6   6

7   7   7

For practitioners
Children practise writing numbers 4, 5, 6 and 7. Children say aloud the numbers they have written.

8, 9, 10!
Write and say.

8 8 8

9 9 9

10 10 10

For practitioners
Children practise writing numbers 8, 9 and 10. Children say aloud the numbers they have written.

Let's paint!
Count and write.

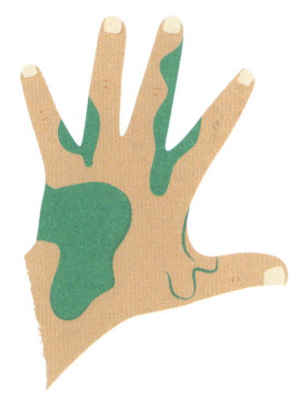

0   1   2   3   4   5

_____   _____

_____   _____

For practitioners
Look at the pictures together. Children count what they see in each picture then write the number on the line.

Money

Match.

Draw a line to the correct number.

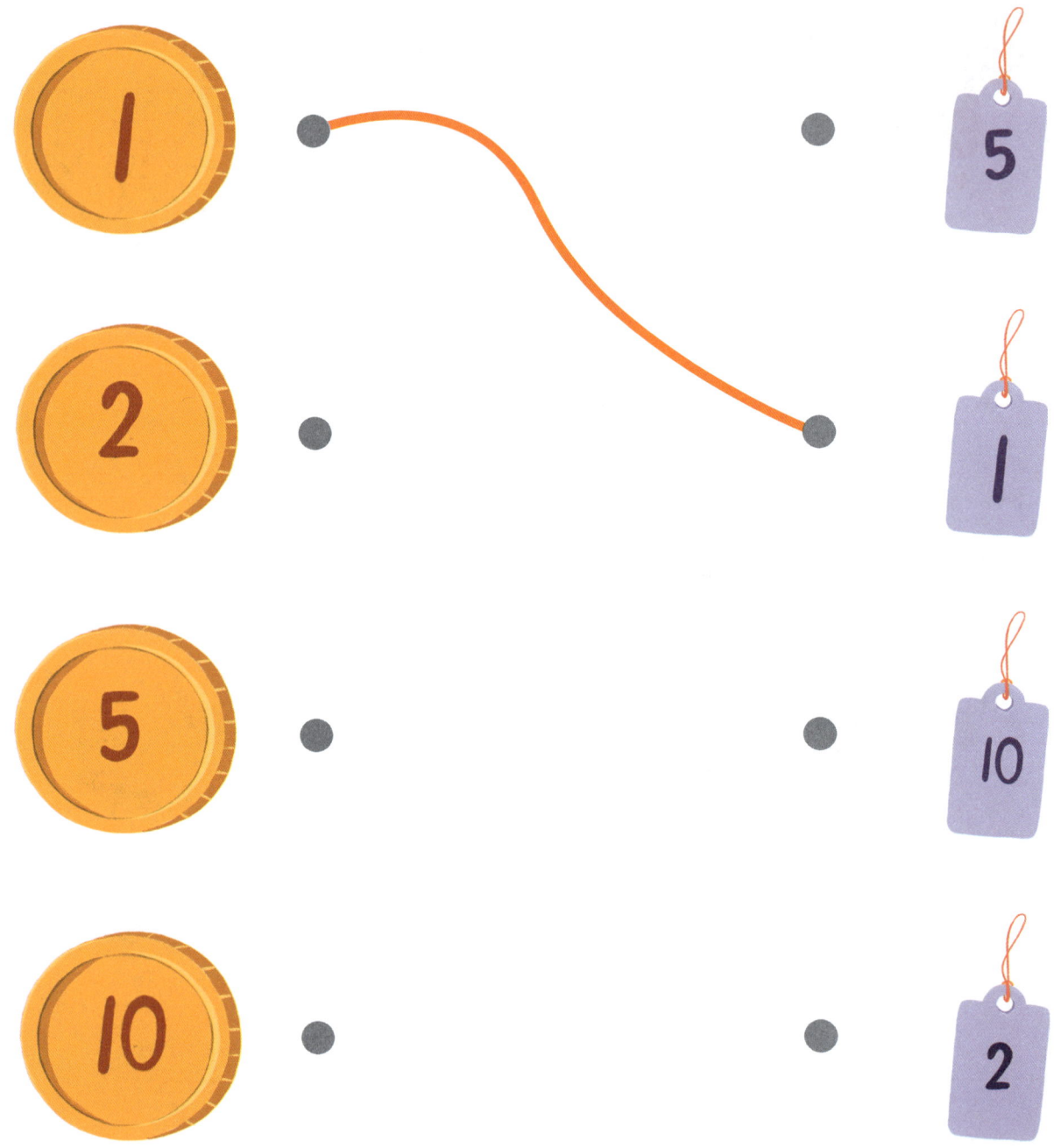

For practitioners
Point to a number and ask the children to read it. The children draw a line to match the numbers.

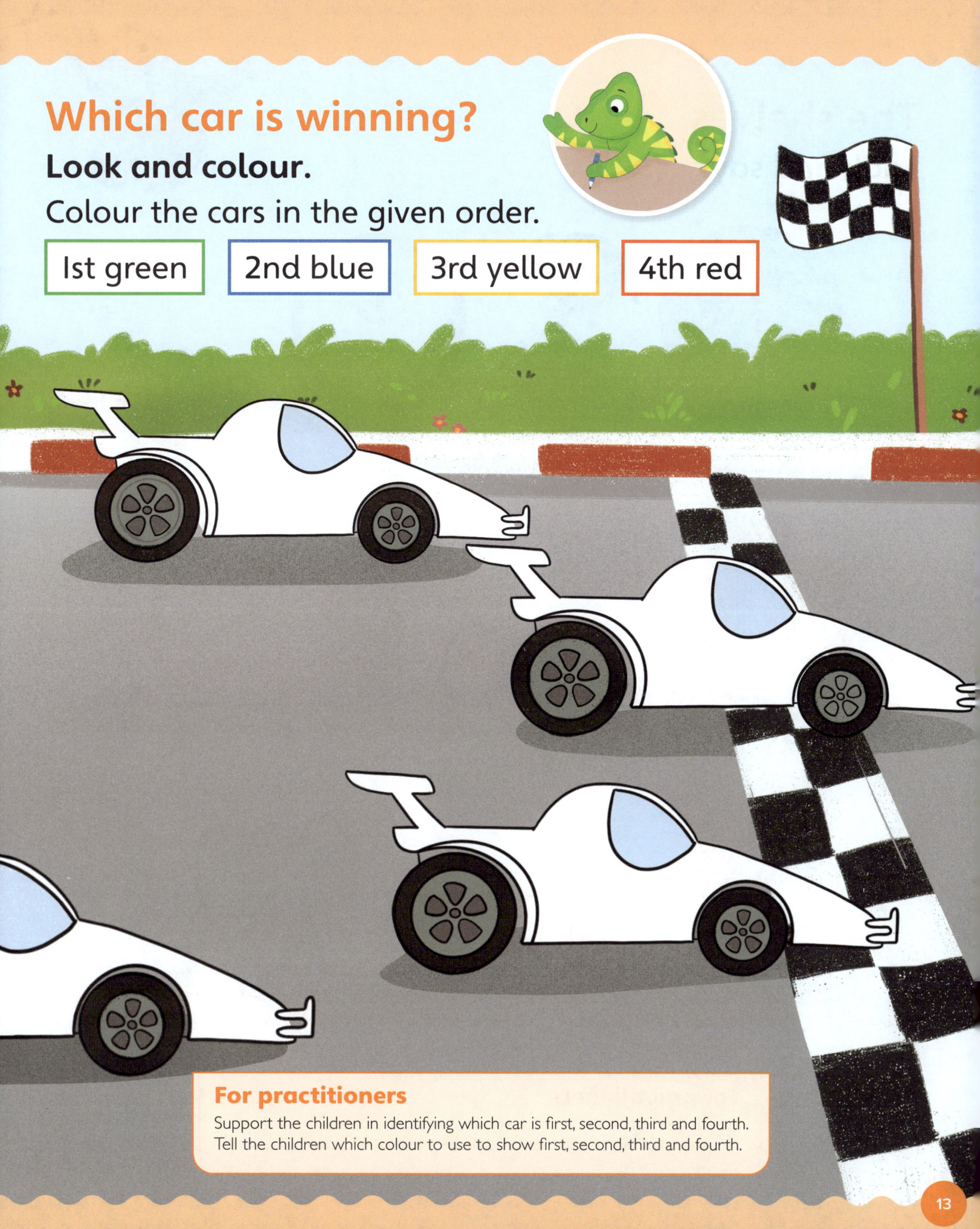

The shelves

Look and say.

For practitioners

Encourage children to discuss the position of each object on the shelves. For example, *The ball is next to the doll. The giraffe is under the books.*

The bedroom

Look and say.

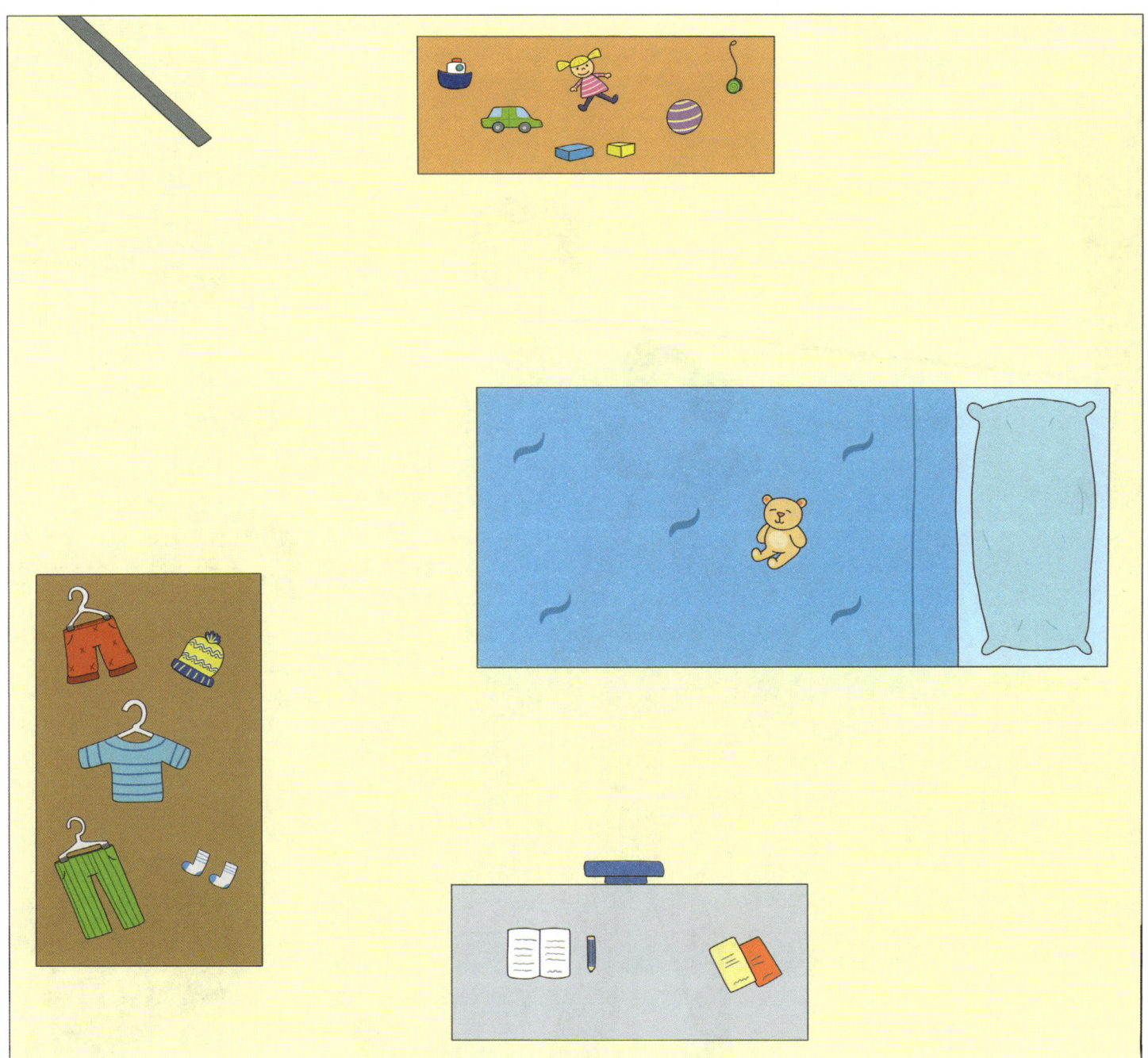

For practitioners
Talk together about what object each picture in the plan represents. Encourage children to discuss the position of each object in the room. For example, *The teddy is on the bed.*

How things move
Look and say.

For practitioners

Children look at the zip wire, slide, seesaw, swings and roundabout. Talk about how they move when using them, e.g. a straight line for a zip wire, up and down on a seesaw, turn/rotate on the roundabout.

Block 2 Home and buildings

In the rainforest
Count and write.

For practitioners
Look at the jungle scene together. Children count the animals and write the number in each box.

Under the sea!
Draw.

 2

 8

 4

For practitioners
Look at the pictures and encourage children to say the numbers aloud. Children draw the matching number of items in each box.

Missing numbers

Write and say.

Missing steps

Draw and say.

Count the steps.
Draw the missing steps and say the number.

For practitioners
Help the children to count the number of steps in each column, starting from the first step.
After the third column, ask them what they think the number of steps in the next column should be.

One more …
Draw and say.

For practitioners
Explain that it's Teddy's party. Children count the presents. Ask children to draw <u>one more</u> present for Teddy in the box provided. Say *Teddy has one more present. How many presents does Teddy have now?* Children respond.

One fewer ...
Tick.

For practitioners
Children tick the picture from each pair that has one fewer.

Days of the week

Tick.

Tick which days of the week you come to school.

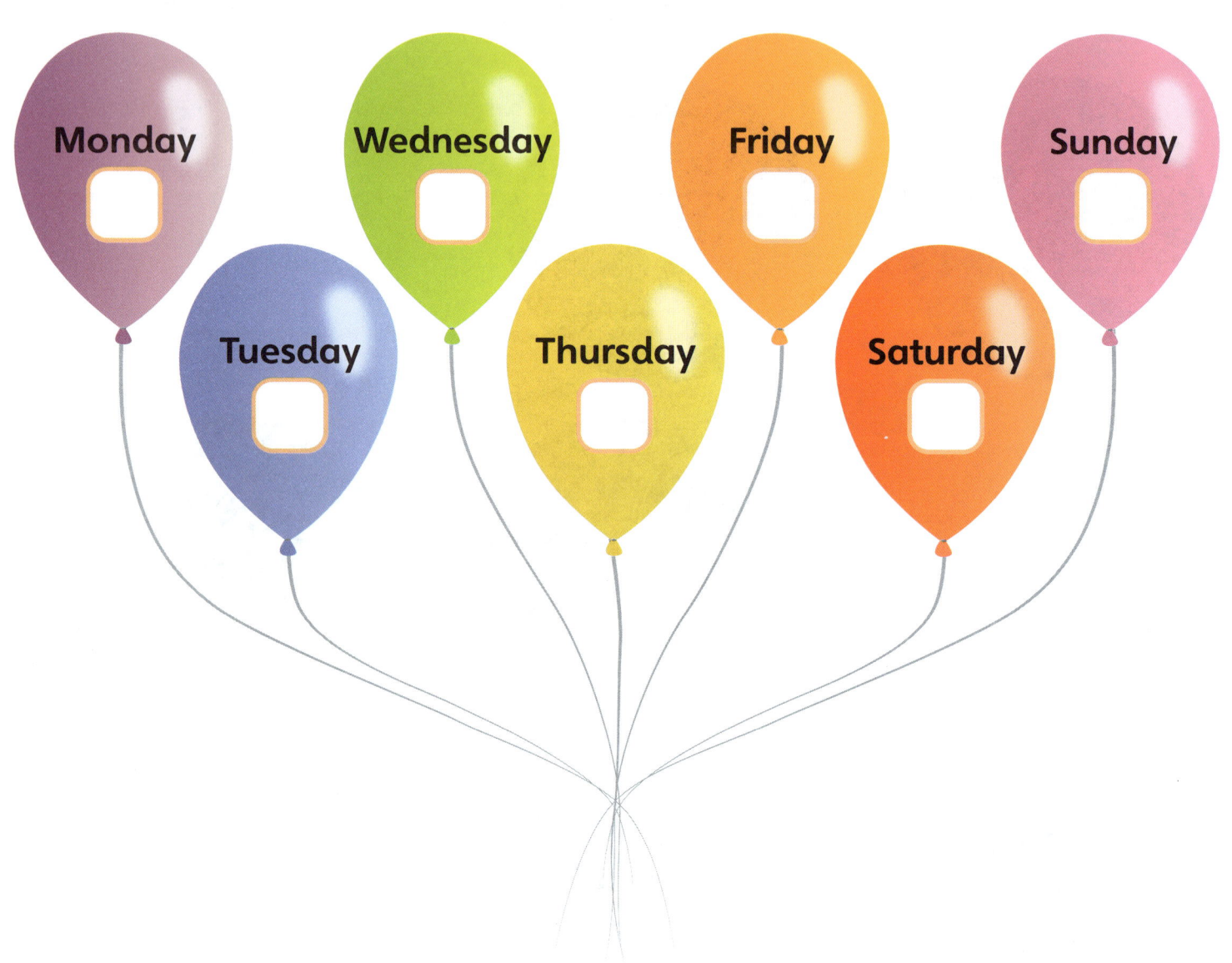

For practitioners
Talk through the days of the week together. Children tick in the boxes for which days of the week they go to school. Ask children what they like to do at the weekend.

When in the day ... ?
Match and say.

Evening

Morning

Afternoon

> **For practitioners**
> Children match the time of day to the activity by drawing lines between the dots. Encourage them to discuss what *they* do in the morning, afternoon and evening.

What is the time?
Write and say.

For practitioners
Children fill in the blanks on the clock. Ask *What is the time on the clock?*

What I do at the weekend

Draw and say.

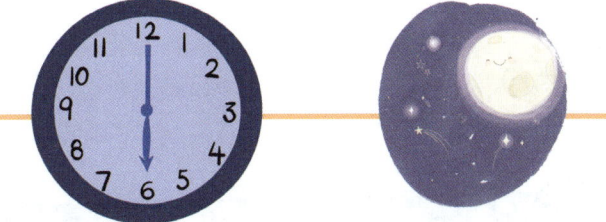

For practitioners
Encourage children to draw and talk about what they might be doing at these times at the weekend.

Where are the clocks?
Circle.

For practitioners

Children circle the clocks they can see in the picture.
Encourage children to tell the time in the picture using any of the clocks.

Acknowledgements

The authors and publishers acknowledge the following sources of copyright material and are grateful for the permissions granted. While every effort has been made, it has not always been possible to identify the sources of all the material used, or to trace all copyright holders. If any omissions are brought to our notice, we will be happy to include the appropriate acknowledgements on reprinting.

Thanks to the following artists at Beehive Illustration:

Laura Arias, Lays Bittencourt, Helen Graper, Alice Larsson, John Lund, Michelle McGovern, Nadene Neude, Nathalie Ortega, Sarah Pitt.

Cover characters by Becky Davies (The Bright Agency)